# Lebanon: Background and U.S. Relations

Casey L. Addis
Analyst in Middle Eastern Affairs

February 1, 2011

Congressional Research Service

7-5700

www.crs.gov

R40054

**CRS Report for Congress** ————————————————

*Prepared for Members and Committees of Congress*

# Summary

Lebanon is a religiously diverse country transitioning toward independence and democratic consolidation after a ruinous civil war and the subsequent Syrian and Israeli occupations. The United States and Lebanon have historically enjoyed a good relationship due in part to cultural and religious ties; the democratic character of the state; a large, Lebanese-American community in the United States; and the pro-western orientation of Lebanon, particularly during the cold war. Current policy priorities of the United States include strengthening the weak democratic institutions of the state, limiting the influence of Iran, Syria, and others in Lebanon's political process, and countering threats from Hezbollah and other militant groups in Lebanon.

Following Syrian withdrawal from Lebanon in 2005 and the war between Israel and Hezbollah in the summer of 2006, the Bush Administration requested and Congress appropriated a significant increase in U.S. assistance to Lebanon. Since 2006, U.S. assistance to Lebanon has topped $1 billion total over three years, including for the first time U.S. security assistance for the Lebanese Armed Forces (LAF) and Internal Security Forces (ISF) of Lebanon.

Several key issues in U.S.-Lebanon relations could potentially affect future U.S. assistance to Lebanon. The scope and influence of foreign actors, primarily Syria and Iran; unresolved territorial disputes; concerns about extremist groups operating in Lebanon; and potential indictments by the Special Tribunal for Lebanon (STL) are among the challenges facing the Lebanese government and U.S. objectives in Lebanon.

On November 9, 2009, five months after the parliamentary elections, Prime Minister Hariri announced that consensus had been reached and a cabinet had been formed. Since then, Hariri has faced the challenging task of governing in an environment where sectarian tensions, political jockeying, and external actors penetrate deeply and often paralyze the day-to-day functions of government. The United States has thrown its support behind the Hariri government in an effort to build state institutions in an attempt to counter those destabilizing forces.

Current U.S. policy toward Lebanon centers on containing Iran's sphere of influence while maintaining security and stability in the Levant. As regional actors like Saudi Arabia, Iran, and Syria continue to compete for influence in the region, Lebanon has become the staging ground for a proxy war that exacerbates historic sectarian tensions and holds hostage the functions of state institutions. The extent to which Prime Minister Hariri's government, bolstered by U.S. support, can overcome these challenges and move toward fully functioning state institutions also depends on the ability of the LAF and United Nations Interim Force in Lebanon (UNIFIL) to keep the peace along Lebanon's southern border with Israel and the willingness of Lebanon's neighbors to limit activities that undermine the Hariri government.

This report provides an overview of Lebanese politics, recent events in Lebanon, and current issues in U.S.-Lebanon relations. For additional information, see CRS Report R40485, *U.S. Security Assistance to Lebanon*, by Casey L. Addis and CRS Report R41446, *Hezbollah: Background and Issues for Congress*, by Casey L. Addis and Christopher M. Blanchard.

# Contents

# Tables

# Appendixes

# Contacts

# Recent Developments

- **Najib Miqati appointed Prime Minister.** On January 25, Hezbollah and its allies nominated former Prime Minister Najib Miqati to replace Hariri as Prime Minister. Miqati was approved by a parliamentary vote of 68 in favor to 60 opposed and is now working to form a new government. Many analysts agree that Miqati's nomination likely came after he agreed to Hezbollah's demands on the STL, and that he will likely support Hezbollah and the opposition on other issues. In response, Hariri's supporters staged a number of protests, and the security situation in Lebanon remains tenuous. Hariri responded by calling for peaceful demonstrations and announcing that he and his allies would not take part in the Hezbollah-backed government, but observers question his resolve.[1] At present, Administration officials appear to be reserving judgment until a new government is formed, a process that could take months. During a press conference in Spain last week, Secretary of State Hillary Clinton said that "…we are watching the situation closely and carefully in Lebanon. We are monitoring new developments. As you know, the government formation is just beginning. A Hezbollah-controlled government would clearly have an impact on our bilateral relationship with Lebanon…[2]

- **Hezbollah, Allies Withdraw from Government.** In anticipation of looming indictments and in response to Prime Minister Hariri's refusal to denounce the STL, Hezbollah and its allies withdrew from the cabinet on January 13, 2011. The resignations coincided with Prime Minister Hariri's meeting with President Obama in Washington. Following the resignations, the White House issued a statement saying that "The efforts by the Hezbollah-led coalition to collapse the Lebanese government only demonstrate their own fear and determination to block the governments ability to conduct its business and advance the aspirations of all of the Lebanese people." The State Department also decried the action, calling it a "transparent effort by forces who seek to subvert justice and undermine Lebanon's stability and progress." According to the constitution, the current government now serves as a caretaker until a new consensus can be reached.

- **Special Tribunal for Lebanon (STL) Indictments.** On January 17, 2011, STL Prosecutor Daniel Bellemare signed indictments against the alleged assassins of Rafiq Hariri and filed them with pre-trial judge Daniel Fransen. Fransen will now review the indictments and reject or certify them. The process could take months and the indictments will remain confidential. Hezbollah responded with organized demonstrations in a number of Beirut neighborhoods, but no serious incidents were reported. Secretary of State Hillary Clinton called this "an important step toward justice and ending impunity for murder." She added that "Those who oppose the Tribunal seek to create a false choice between justice and stability in Lebanon; we reject this."

---

[1] "Hariri Refuses to Join Government Headed by Hizbullah," *Naharnet*, January 24, 2011. See also "After Riots and Rage, Lebanon is ready to move on," *Haaretz.com*, January 27, 2011.

[2] Secretary of State Hillary Clinton's Remarks with Spanish Foreign Minister Jimenez, January 25, 2011.

# U.S. Policy Toward Lebanon

The United States and Lebanon have historically enjoyed a good relationship due in part to cultural and religious ties; the democratic character of the state; a large, Lebanese-American community in the United States; and the pro-western orientation of Lebanon, particularly during the cold war. The American University of Beirut (AUB) was founded in 1866 by Americans in Lebanon and continues to receive U.S. funding.

Despite long-standing interaction between the United States and Lebanon, some might argue that Lebanon is of limited strategic value to the United States. Unlike many American partners in the Middle East, Lebanon has no U.S. military bases, oil fields, international waterways, military or industrial strength, or major trading ties with the United States. Others would disagree, pointing to Lebanon's strategic location as a buffer between Israel and Syria, Lebanon's large Palestinian refugee population, and its historical role as an interlocutor for the United States with the Arab world.

Current U.S. policy toward Lebanon centers on containing Iran's sphere of influence while maintaining security and stability in the Levant. As regional actors like Saudi Arabia, Iran, and Syria compete for influence in the region, Lebanon has become the staging ground for a proxy war that exacerbates historic sectarian tensions and holds hostage the functions of state institutions. The extent to which Prime Minister Hariri's government, bolstered by U.S. support, can overcome these challenges also depends on the willingness of Lebanon's neighbors to limit activities that undermine the government.

## Background[3]

During the 1975-1990 Lebanese civil war, the United States expressed concern over the violence and destruction and provided emergency economic aid, military training, and limited amounts of military equipment. In addition, the United States briefly deployed military forces to Lebanon in the early 1980s. The forces withdrew after a bombing at the U.S. Embassy in April 1983 and a bombing at the U.S. Marine barracks in October 1983 collectively killed 272 civilians and members of the U.S. Armed Forces in Lebanon. The United States supported various efforts to bring about a cease-fire during the civil war and subsequent efforts to quiet unrest in southern Lebanon along the Lebanese-Israeli border.

Since Israel's withdrawal from Lebanon in 2000, U.S. efforts have focused on countering terrorism and promoting democracy, two agendas that sometimes clash in Lebanon as Hezbollah maintains a political party that competes in Lebanon's national and municipal elections, extensive social and educational services, a militia wing, and an overseas terrorist capability.

The Bush Administration reacted strongly to the assassination of former Prime Minister Rafiq Hariri in February 2005, criticized the Syrian presence in Lebanon, and demanded the withdrawal of Syrian forces. The United States welcomed the formation of a new Lebanese government following the withdrawal of Syrian forces in April 2005 and also supported the United Nations in establishing an independent tribunal to prosecute those responsible for Hariri's assassination.

---

[3] For additional background see "Political Profile" section.

Large-scale fighting between Israel and Hezbollah in mid-2006 complicated U.S. policy toward Lebanon.[4] In a broader sense, the conflict jeopardized not only the long-term stability of Lebanon but presented the U.S. government with a basic dilemma. On one hand, the United States was sympathetic to Israeli military action against a terrorist organization. On the other hand, the fighting dealt a setback to U.S. efforts to support the rebuilding of physical infrastructure and democratic institutions in Lebanon. The fighting also served as a reminder of ongoing Syrian and Iranian support to proxies in Lebanon and the possibility of a larger, regional war.

Following the war, Hezbollah, emboldened by increased popular support, began to push for an expanded role in the government. Subsequent internal government disputes led to a vacant presidency and 18 months of political stalemate. The United States watched cautiously while continuing to assist and support the March 14[5] coalition until January 23, 2007, when Hezbollah called a general strike aimed at toppling the government. In response, then-Under Secretary of State Nicholas Burns called on Arabs and Europeans to throw their support behind then-Lebanese Prime Minister Siniora against those who would try to destabilize his regime. Following the Doha Agreement[6] in May 2008 that ended the stalemate, then-Secretary of State Condoleezza Rice reiterated U.S. support for the government of Lebanon and its "complete authority over the entire territory of the country."

The Obama Administration has supported the current government, elected in June 2009 and led by Prime Minister Saad Hariri. Hezbollah has maintained its role in the government and continued to expand its influence in Lebanese politics. Iranian President Mahmoud Ahmadinejad's October 2010 visit to Lebanon signaled strong support for its proxy in the face of continued U.S. and international efforts to peel Lebanon away from Iran and Syria.

As the Obama Administration and the 112th Congress reevaluate U.S. policy in the region, the U.S. approach toward Lebanon could become a harbinger of a new direction or a continuation of the status quo. While the United States wants to promote stability and curb Syrian and Iranian influence in Lebanon, there is a debate over how best to achieve these goals. The United States could continue its support for the March 14 coalition government, promoting democracy and stability with economic and security assistance. Another alternative is to address the situation in Lebanon as part of a larger regional initiative, possibly one that centers on Syria, Israel, and the peace process. However, events may ultimately dictate a U.S. course of action in Lebanon, particularly in the coming months as the international community works to dissuade Iran from a nuclear weapon and the STL prepares to issue indictments.

## Recent U.S. Assistance to Lebanon

In recent years, the United States has increased its economic and military assistance to Lebanon. After Syria withdrew its forces from Lebanon in 2005, the United States increased assistance to support the moderate March 14 government. The summer 2006 war between Hezbollah and Israel

---

[4] For additional information see CRS Report RL33566, *Lebanon: The Israel-Hamas-Hezbollah Conflict*, coordinated by Jeremy M. Sharp.

[5] The March 14 coalition is led by Prime-Minister Designate Saad Hariri and his Sunni party Future Movement. The opposition March 8 Alliance is led by the Shiite party Amal and the Maronite Christian Free Patriotic Movement. It also includes Hezbollah.

[6] The full text of the Doha Agreement is available at http://www.nowlebanon.com/NewsArchiveDetails.aspx?ID=44023.

heightened the need for additional economic aid, as the Lebanese government and its international and Arab partners vied with Iran and Hezbollah to win the hearts and minds of many Lebanese citizens who lost homes and businesses.

The FY2007 Emergency Supplemental Appropriations Act (P.L. 110-28, adopted May 25, 2007) provided more than $580 million in security and economic assistance to support Lebanon's recovery and to strengthen the Lebanese security forces (see "Security Assistance," below). The supplemental also provided $184 million in Contributions for International Peacekeeping Activities (CIPA) funding for Lebanon. Appropriations for FY2008, FY2009, and FY2010 and the FY2011 request support the continuation of these efforts, albeit at lower levels.

For more information on U.S. economic and security assistance to Lebanon, see "U.S. Assistance to Lebanon," below.

### Table I. Recent U.S. Assistance to Lebanon (FY2006-FY2011)

(regular and supplemental appropriations; current year $ in millions)

| Account | FY2006 | FY2007a | FY2008 | FY2009a | FY2010 (estimate) | FY2011 (request) |
|---|---|---|---|---|---|---|
| ESF | $39.60 | $334.00 | $44.64 | $67.50 | $109.00 | $109.00 |
| FMF | $30.00 | $224.80 | $6.94 | $159.70 | $100.00 | $100.00 |
| INCLE | — | $60.00 | $0.50 | $6.00 | $20.00 | $30.00 |
| NADR | $2.98 | $8.50 | $4.75 | $4.60 | $6.80 | $4.80 |
| 1206 (DOD) | $10.60 | $30.60 | $15.10 | $49.24 | $33.60 | — |
| IMET | $0.75 | $0.91 | $1.20 | $2.28 | $2.50 | $2.50 |
| CIPA | — | $184.00 | — | — | — | — |
| DA | $2.00 | — | — | — | — | — |
| Total | $86.21 | $843.85 | $73.13 | $125.70 | $229.00 | $246.30 |

**Source:** U.S. Department of State, Congressional Budget Justifications for Foreign Operations. Includes funds from the following accounts: Economic Support Fund (ESF), Foreign Military Financing (FMF), International Narcotics Control and Law Enforcement Assistance (INCLE), Non-proliferation, Anti-terrorism, De-mining, and Related funding (NADR), International Military and Education Training (IMET),Contributions for International Peacekeeping Activities (CIPA) and Development Assistance (DA). Funding for "1206" refers to the Department of Defense Global Train and Equip program, originally authorized by Section 1206 of the National Defense Authorization Act for Fiscal Year 2006 (P.L. 109-163).

a.    FY2007 and FY2009 numbers include regular and supplemental appropriations.

# Current Issues in U.S.-Lebanon Relations

## Hezbollah[7]

Syrian and Iranian backing of Hezbollah, an organization that has committed terrorist acts against U.S. personnel and facilities and has sworn to eliminate Israel, is perhaps the greatest obstacle to U.S. efforts to bolster the pro-Western forces in Lebanon. With Hezbollah deeply entrenched in Lebanese Shiite society, the movement has become a fixture in the Lebanese political system and a symbol of resistance against Israel for many in the region. This dual identity has benefitted Hezbollah, and there have been no recent indications that it is willing to renounce violence and become solely a Lebanese political movement. There also is little evidence to suggest that Iran and Hezbollah's strategic relationship could be severed despite the fact that Hezbollah's agenda may be more nationalist while Iran's may be more revolutionary pan-Shiite. Though some analysts argue that Hezbollah has grown more independent of Tehran since the 1980s, Hezbollah still requires advanced weaponry and outside funding, while Iran requires a proxy to pressure Israel and the United States. Both parties have found this relationship to be mutually beneficial.

At present, clear solutions to the challenges that Hezbollah poses to Lebanon, Israel, and the United States are not evident. Administration reports state that Hezbollah has rearmed and expanded its arsenal in defiance of United Nations Security Council resolutions and in spite of international efforts to prevent the smuggling of weaponry from Iran and Syria. Lebanese border and maritime security capabilities remain nascent, and long-standing political conflicts continue to prevent the clear delineation of boundaries between Lebanon, Syria, and Israel. Administration reports state that Iran continues to provide Hezbollah with weapons, training, and financing, thereby sustaining the organization's ability to field an effective military force that threatens Israel's security and the sovereignty of the Lebanese government. Hezbollah's electoral success in the 2009 national elections and its seats in Lebanon's cabinet complicate U.S. and other international efforts to engage with Beirut on security issues and a number of key reform questions. Lebanon's domestic political environment appears fractured by sectarian and political rivalries, and its leaders remain at an impasse with regard to the overarching questions of the country's security needs and the future of Hezbollah's weapons.

### Weapons Smuggling to Hezbollah and Alleged Missile Transfers

In early April 2010, multiple reports surfaced suggesting that Syria may have transferred Scud missiles to Hezbollah.[8] Syria denied the charges. Unnamed U.S. officials have acknowledged that they believe that Syria intended to transfer long-range missiles to Hezbollah, "but there are doubts about whether the Scuds were delivered in full and whether they were moved to Lebanon."[9] The State Department issued a statement saying, "The United States condemns in the strongest terms the transfer of any arms, and especially ballistic missile systems such as the Scud, from Syria to Hezbollah.... The transfer of these arms can only have a destabilizing effect on the

---

[7] For additional information, see CRS Report R41446, *Hezbollah: Background and Issues for Congress*, by Casey L. Addis and Christopher M. Blanchard.

[8] U.S. Open Source Center (OSC) Report GMP20100411184001, "Syria Sends Scud Missiles to Hizballah, Israel Threatens War," *Al Ra'y* Online (Kuwait), April 11, 2010.

[9] "U.S. Says Unclear if Hezbollah Took Scuds to Lebanon," Reuters, April 16, 2010.

region, and would pose an immediate threat to both the security of Israel and the sovereignty of Lebanon."[10] Subsequent Israeli press reports have cited Israeli military officials as stating that the missiles transferred to date have been M-600s, a ballistic missile with a 185-mile range and half-ton payload.[11]

Hezbollah leaders deny allegations that they have transferred weapons south of the Litani River in violation of Resolution 1701.[12] Nevertheless, U.N. reporting has noted Israel's stated concerns about the use of private homes in southern Lebanon to store weapons and explosives belonging to Hezbollah. Explosions at suspected weapons caches in south Lebanon in July and October 2009 and the discovery of over 600 pounds of explosives near the Israeli-Lebanon border in December 2009 appeared to substantiate general concerns that illegal weaponry continues to enter and circulate in southern Lebanon, in spite of United Nations Interim Force in Lebanon (UNIFIL) and the Lebanese Armed Forces (LAF) presence in the area.

## Special Tribunal for Lebanon

More than five years after the assassination of Prime Minister Rafiq Hariri, the Special Tribunal for Lebanon (STL)[13] at The Hague, Netherlands, has yet to issue indictments against any alleged perpetrators. The only suspects ever named in the ongoing investigation, a group of four generals who headed Lebanon's security services at the time of the assassination and were detained in 2005, were released in 2009. According to one Lebanese observer, "Foreign governments fear the instability that might ensue if Mr. Bellemare [STL Chief Prosecutor] issues indictments, so few will regret it if he doesn't. But the United Nations pushed for the Hariri investigation; its integrity is tied up with a plausible outcome. If that's impossible, there is no point in insulting the victims by letting the charade continue."[14] In March 2010, STL Prosecutor Daniel Bellemare questioned several Hezbollah officials, including Hajj Salim, who heads the Special Operations Department, Mustafa Badreddine, head of the counter-intelligence unit, and Wafiq Safa, chief of security.[15] As a result, numerous media reports have speculated that high-ranking members of Hezbollah may be indicted.[16]

In anticipation of possible indictments, Hezbollah has mounted a public relations campaign aimed at discrediting the tribunal and intimidating the tribunal's supporters. From 2009 to 2010 Lebanese security forces arrested dozens of Lebanese citizens and government officials, many of whom worked in or had access to the telecommunications sector, on charges of spying for Israel. Hezbollah's leadership has sought to link the alleged spy networks with a broader scheme to

---

[10] "U.S. Speaks to Syrian Envoy of Arms Worries," *New York Times*, April 19, 2010.

[11] Jonathan Lis and Amos Harel, "Syria gave advanced M-600 missiles to Hezbollah, defense officials claim," *Haaretz* (Israel), May 5, 2010.

[12] United Nations Security Council 1701 (August 11, 2006) called for, among other things, the full cessation of hostilities between Israel and Hezbollah, Israeli withdrawal from southern Lebanon in parallel with the deployment of LAF and UNIFIL to the area, and the disarmament of all groups in Lebanon other than the LAF and ISF. The full text of the Resolution is available at http://daccess-dds-ny.un.org/doc/UNDOC/GEN/N06/465/03/PDF/N0646503.pdf? OpenElement.

[13] For additional background, see "U.N. Resolutions 1595, 1757, and the Tribunal" below.

[14] "All fall down," *The Middle East*, May 1, 2010.

[15] Op. cit.

[16] "UN Hariri court to file charges by year's end," *Middle East Online*, May 17, 2010.

---

exploit the STL investigation to create discord in Lebanon.[17] On August 9, 2010, Nasrallah held a press conference in which he claimed to have evidence that implicates Israel in the Hariri assassination. He also characterized the STL as an "Israeli project" and called for an internal Lebanese commission to investigate the assassination. He said:

> We have definite information on the aerial movements of the Israeli enemy the day Hariri was murdered. Hours before he was murdered, an Israeli drone was surveying the Sidon-Beirut-Jounieh coastline as warplanes were flying over Beirut.... This video can be acquired by any investigative commission to ensure it is correct. We are sure of this evidence or else we would not risk showing it.... However, if the Lebanese government is willing to form a Lebanese commission to investigate the matter, we will cooperate.... There are some who spent $500 million in Lebanon to distort the image of Hezbollah. That's why we're engaging ourselves in a battle for public opinion, especially that some are working night and day to defend Israel's innocence.[18]

Since his address, the March 14 coalition and the opposition have exchanged criticisms in the press, and recent statements have led some observers to speculate that Hezbollah's media campaign may be affecting the March 14 coalition and Prime Minister Hariri's commitment to the process. In an interview with *As-Sharq Al-Awsat* on September 6, 2010, Hariri appeared to walk back his accusation that Syria is responsible, a position that he had maintained since 2005:

> I have opened a new page in relations with Syria since the formation of the government.... One must be realistic in this relationship and build it on solid foundations. One should also assess the past years, so as not to repeat previous mistakes. Hence, we conducted an assessment of errors committed on our behalf with Syria, and I felt for the Syrian people, and the relationship between the two countries. We must always look at the interest of both peoples, both countries and their relationship. At a certain stage we made mistakes. We accused Syria of assassinating the martyred premier, and this was a political accusation.... I do not want to talk much about the tribunal, but I will say that the tribunal is not linked to the political accusations, which were hasty.

Hariri's statements have raised concerns that the political costs of supporting the STL may be increasing, and that Hezbollah and the opposition's campaign has upped the ante for indictments. Some analysts have questioned whether they will be issued at all. Bellemare has repeatedly stated that he will not allow the investigation to be influenced by Lebanese politics, "I am not influenced by what is said on TV. If I was to gauge my investigation along this, then I would be politicized. I have to go through the steps to make sure the result is a credible (step). And that the people—the victims and their relatives—will have an outcome they are able to believe."[19] U.N. Secretary-General Ban Ki-moon responded to the recent exchanges between Hariri and Nasrallah by saying that he does not believe that the future of the STL is at stake: "The Special Tribunal on Lebanon has been working and making progress. This is an independent judiciary process, so that should not be linked with any political remarks by whomever, by any politicians."

---

[17] OSC Report GMP20100721966025, "The Daily Star: Baroud Refuses to Take Part in Debate Over Spy Probes," *The Daily Star Online*, July 21, 2010.

[18] OSC Report GMP20100810637004, "Al-Manar: Sayyed Nasrallah: Israel Behind Hariri's Assassination," *Beirut Al-Manar TV Online*, August 10, 2010

[19] OSC Report GMP20100908966046, "Rare Bellemare, An Assessment," *Beirut NOW Lebanon*, September 8, 2010.

# Lebanon-Syria Relations

Most analysts agree that Syrian interference is the single greatest hindrance to Lebanon's independence and stability. A cornerstone of Syrian foreign policy is to dominate the internal affairs of Lebanon.[20] For many hard-line Syrian politicians, Lebanon is considered an appendage of the Syrian state and, until recently, Syria never formally recognized Lebanon. From a geostrategic standpoint, Lebanon is considered by the Syrian government to be a buffer between Syria and Israel. The Lebanese economy also is deeply penetrated by pro-Syrian business interests.

Between 2008 and 2009, Syria improved its relationships with France and Saudi Arabia, established diplomatic relations with Lebanon for the first time in history, and refrained from overtly manipulating the June 2009 Lebanese elections. During this period its position in Lebanese politics has strengthened, which, in turn, has forced some anti-Syrian Lebanese leaders to reassess policies toward their more powerful neighbor.

Prime Minster Saad Hariri has had to accommodate his political positions to new regional realities, even though his father was assassinated in a plot that many observers believe was hatched by Syrian leaders. With one of the Hariri family's primary benefactors, Saudi Arabia, no longer openly hostile toward Syria, and with the Obama Administration supporting more fulsome diplomatic relations with Syria, Prime Minister Hariri's room to maneuver has diminished. Consequently, he has now made two trips to Damascus for meetings with Syrian President Basher al Asad, and both sides have spoken positively about turning a new page in Syrian-Lebanese relations.

Despite the public display of amity between the two leaders, Syria continues to act in ways that many view as undermining Lebanese sovereignty. For example, the demarcation of a common border between Lebanon and Syria remains unresolved, an issue some attribute to Syrian complacency or obstruction. The joint visit of Iranian President Mahmoud Ahmadinejad and Hezbollah Secretary General Nasrallah to Damascus in February 2010 also cast doubt on the willingness of Syrian leaders to fundamentally shift their positions regarding Lebanese sovereignty and security. President Suleiman's June 2010 visit to Damascus reportedly focused on border demarcation, but did not result in an announced agreement. Prime Minister Hariri visited Syria on July 18, 2010. According to reports, the visit was amicable. The two governments signed a total of 17 accords covering justice, tourism, education and agriculture and pledged to continue to cooperate to secure their common border to combat smuggling and other illicit activities.[21] On July 30, 2010, Syrian President Basher al-Assad visited Beirut along with His Majesty Abdullah bin Abd al Aziz Al Saud of Saudi Arabia. Observers have speculated that the unprecedented joint visit bodes well for Lebanon, signaling ongoing normalization between Syria and Lebanon as well as entente between Syria and Saudi Arabia, whose Shiite/Sunni power politics are often played out at the expense of Lebanese stability.[22]

The recess appointment of U.S. Ambassador Robert Ford to Damascus in December 2010 raised concerns among some observers that U.S. engagement with Syria undermines U.S. support for an

---

[20] For additional information see CRS Report RL33487, *Syria: Issues for the 112th Congress and Background on U.S. Sanctions*, by Jeremy M. Sharp.

[21] "Lebanon, Syria Sign String of Accords," *Middle East Online*, July 19, 2010.

[22] Jim Muir, "Syrian and Saudi leaders visit Beirut to defuse tension," *BBC News*, July 30, 2010.

independent Lebanon. On the other hand, some analysts argue that U.S. engagement with Syria and, most of all, peace between Israel and Syria are lynchpins of Lebanese independence and stability. Syria considers Lebanon a buffer between itself and Israel, and only if the tension between Israel and Syria were resolved might Syria feel secure enough to respect Lebanese sovereignty.[23]

## U.S. Assistance to the Lebanese Armed Forces (LAF)

On August 3, 2010, the LAF opened fire on an Israeli Defense Force (IDF) unit engaged in routine brush-clearing maintenance along the Blue Line, alleging that it had crossed over into Lebanese territory. Two Lebanese soldiers, a journalist, and an Israeli officer were killed in the confrontation. Soon after the incident, UNIFIL issued a report confirming that the IDF had not been in Lebanese territory. Although incidents along the Blue Line[24] are not uncommon, UNIFIL called this incident the "most serious" along the border since 2006.

In response, Congresswoman Nita Lowey, then-Chairwoman of the State Foreign Operations Subcommittee of the House Committee on Appropriations placed a hold on the FY2010 $100 million FMF appropriation for Lebanon citing the need to "determine whether equipment that the United States provided to the Lebanese Armed Forces was used against our ally, Israel." Prior to the incident on August 3, Congressman Howard Berman, then-Chairman of the House Foreign Affairs Committee, also placed a hold on the FY2010 assistance, pending a better understanding from the State Department about the strategy for U.S. assistance to Lebanon and assurances that the LAF is a responsible actor. Other Members also publicly expressed concerns. The hold was lifted in November following congressional consultations with the State Department. It is unclear how these concerns will impact congressional consideration of the Administration's FY2011 request for Lebanon.

For additional information, see "Security Assistance," below.

## Unresolved Territorial Disputes

### The Shib'a Farms[25]

Israel's withdrawal from southern Lebanon in 2000 left several small but sensitive territorial issues unresolved. The most prominent example is a 10-square-mile enclave called the Shib'a Farms (alternate spelling: Shebaa) located at the Lebanese-Israeli-Syrian tri-border area (see **Appendix B**). Many third parties, notably the United Nations, maintain that the Shib'a Farms is part of the Israeli-occupied Syrian Golan Heights and is not part of the Lebanese territory from which Israel was required to withdraw. Lebanon, supported by Syria, asserts that this territory is

---

[23] For additional information, see CRS Report RL33487, *Syria: Issues for the 112th Congress and Background on U.S. Sanctions*, by Jeremy M. Sharp.

[24] The Blue Line is the line of Israeli withdrawal recognized by the United Nations in 2000. It is not the Israeli-Lebanese border.

[25] For additional information see CRS Report RL31078, *The Shib'a Farms Dispute and Its Implications*, by Alfred B. Prados.

part of Lebanon and should have been evacuated by Israel. In a June 2008 interview, Prime Minister Siniora said that "the demand to restore sovereignty to Shib'a is a Lebanese demand."[26]

Hezbollah has consistently used Israel's presence in the Shib'a Farms as justification for retaining its weapons and refusing to disarm. Until recently, Israel refused to negotiate a withdrawal from the area. However, in June 2008, against the backdrop of prisoner exchange negotiations with Hezbollah and indirect peace talks with Syria, Israel shifted its position and, in mid-June, then-Secretary of State Condoleezza Rice stated that "the time has come to deal with the Shebaa Farms issue." The most recent report of the U.N. Secretary General to the Security Council on the implementation of Resolution 1701 stated that Syria and Lebanon have agreed to reactivate the taskforce charged with delineating their common border and that Syria recognized the Shib'a as part of the territory of Lebanon.[27] The work of the taskforce has since stagnated.

## Ghajar

Ghajar is a divided village on the border between Israel and Lebanon. Israel took over the southern part of the village more than 40 years ago and annexed it 14 years later. Israel took over the northern area from Lebanon in 2006. Israeli withdrawal from Northern Ghajar is one among a number of outstanding provisions of UNSCR 1701. Israeli troops and civilians remain north of the Blue Line in Northern Ghajar. Lebanon has agreed to a United Nations-brokered withdrawal plan whereby UNIFIL will replace Israeli troops pending the relocation of northern Ghajar residents. Israel has committed to resolving the issue, but is debating whether to adopt the U.N. plan or withdraw its troops and citizens en masse.

Analysts have argued that Israeli withdrawal from Ghajar could bolster popular support for UNIFIL and demonstrate the ability of the force to fulfill its mandate. Most agree that Ghajar withdrawal is a necessary first step toward a comprehensive Middle East peace process that includes Lebanon. Ghajar negotiations via Israel-UNIFIL-Lebanon trilateral meetings in the southern Lebanese town of Naqoura and U.N. shuttle diplomacy are the only instance of Israeli-Lebanese diplomatic engagement, albeit indirect.

# United Nations Interim Force in Lebanon (UNIFIL)

The U.N. Interim Force in Lebanon (UNIFIL) was created in 1978 to monitor Israel's withdrawal from Lebanese territory as called for in Security Council Resolutions 425 and 426.[28] The size of the force has changed over the last 30 years, and, at the time of the 2006 Israel-Hezbollah war, the force was made up of almost 2,000 military personnel from eight countries.[29] Resolution 1701

---

[26] U.S. Open Source Center (OSC) Document –GMP20080620644012, "Lebanon: Excerpt of Siniora's Remarks on Shab'a Farms, Hisballah Weapons," *Lebanese National News Agency* (Beirut), June 20, 2008.

[27] U.N. Security Council Document S/2008/715, "Report of the Secretary-General on the Implementation of Security Council Resolution 1701 (2006)," November 18, 2008.

[28] In March 1978, Israel launched Operation Litani, an invasion of southern Lebanon designed to expel Palestinian terrorist groups from the Lebanese-Israeli border area following a series of cross-border attacks by Palestinians into Israel. Israel withdrew later in 1978, but reinvaded Lebanon in 1982, occupying the area south of the Litani River until May 2000.

[29] "As of 30 June 2006, UNIFIL was comprised 1,990 troops, from China (187); France (209), Ghana (648), India (673), Ireland (5), Italy (53), Poland (214) and Ukraine (1).... In addition, UNIFIL employed 408 civilian staff, of whom 102 were recruited internationally and 306 locally." U.N. Security Council Document S/2006/560, "Report of (continued...)

---

expanded the authorized size of the UNIFIL force to a maximum of 15,000 personnel and empowered it to monitor the cessation of hostilities; to deploy to southern Lebanon alongside the LAF; to ensure humanitarian access to southern Lebanon; and to assist the LAF in establishing a zone free of non-LAF weapons, military personnel, and assets between the Blue Line and the Litani River. Further, Resolution 1701 empowers UNIFIL, if requested by the Lebanese government, to assist in securing Lebanese borders and entry points against the entry of unauthorized weaponry. In support of this expanded mandate, the Security Council has authorized UNIFIL

> to take all necessary action in areas of deployment of its forces and as it deems within its capabilities, to ensure that its area of operations is not utilized for hostile activities of any kind, to resist attempts by forceful means to prevent it from discharging its duties under the mandate of the Security Council, and to protect United Nations personnel, facilities, installations and equipment, ensure the security and freedom of movement of United Nations personnel, humanitarian workers and, without prejudice to the responsibility of the Government of Lebanon, to protect civilians under imminent threat of physical violence.

UNIFIL personnel work closely with LAF counterparts in carrying out their mandate through joint training and patrol operations, mine clearance, and coordination and liaison meetings. As of November 30, 2010, UNIFIL's deployed force consisted of 11,819 military personnel from 33 countries (see **Table 2**, below). These forces work alongside the 6,400 LAF forces deployed in the UNIFIL area of operations. A UNIFIL Maritime Task Force has assisted Lebanese forces in providing maritime security since 2006: UNIFIL reports that to date over 470 vessels have been referred to Lebanese forces for investigation out of over 28,000 that have been hailed at sea by international forces. At present, the Task Force consists of ships from Germany (3), Greece (1), Italy (1), and Turkey (1) and operates under Italian command.[30] Spanish Army Major-General Alberto Asarta Cuevas has served as the overall UNIFIL Force Commander since January 2010. In February 2010, the U.N. Secretary General reported on the results of a comprehensive review of UNIFIL operations and noted several recommendations to improve the mobility and capability of the UNIFIL force and strengthen its liaison and assistance contributions.[31] The Secretary General also warned that "the current deployment, assets and resources of UNIFIL cannot be sustained indefinitely."

---

(...continued)

the Secretary-General on the United Nations Interim Force in Lebanon," July 21, 2006.

[30] To date, Belgium, Bulgaria, Denmark, France, Germany, Greece, Indonesia, Italy, the Netherlands, Norway, Spain, Sweden and Turkey have contributed ships on a rotating basis to the UNIFIL Maritime Task Force.

[31] United Nations Security Council Document S/2010/86, "Letter dated 12 February 2010 from the Secretary-General to the President of the Security Council," February 16, 2010.

## Table 2. UNIFIL Force Contingents

(as of November 30, 2010)

| | | |
|---|---|---|
| Bangladesh - 325 | France - 1,425 | Korea - 368 |
| Belarus - 1 | FYR Macedonia - 1 | Malaysia - 793 |
| Belgium - 104 | Germany - 233 | Nepal - 1,020 |
| Brazil - 1 | Ghana - 877 | Nigeria - 1 |
| Brunei - 19 | Greece - 54 | Portugal - 15 |
| Cambodia - 215 | Guatemala - 2 | Qatar - 3 |
| China - 344 | Hungary - 4 | Sierra Leone - 3 |
| Croatia - 1 | India - 897 | Slovenia - 14 |
| Cyprus - 2 | Indonesia - 1,417 | Spain - 1,075 |
| Denmark - 125 | Ireland - 9 | Tanzania - 78 |
| El Salvador - 52 | Italy - 1,720 | Turkey - 481 |

**Source:** UNIFIL Contingents, available at http://unifil.unmissions.org/Default.aspx?tabid=1504.

## Lebanon, Iran, and United Nations Sanctions

Lebanon held the rotating presidency of the United Nations Security Council in May 2010 as a non-permanent member and abstained from the recent vote on sanctions against Iran contained in Resolution 1929. Hezbollah holds two seats in the Lebanese cabinet and rejects sanctions against its primary benefactor. According to Lebanese Ambassador to the United Nations Nawwaf Salam:

> Lebanon encourages a peaceful solution to the crisis with Iran. We refuse to imagine a failure to diplomacy. If the current diplomatic efforts fail, our response will be a call for more diplomatic efforts. There are still many opportunities, and we have to secure all means of success for them through support for the mediation of the Brazilian president and the efforts of Turkey. If these efforts do not work, new doors for diplomacy should be opened. This is our position.[32]

# U.S. Assistance to Lebanon

The United States has long provided foreign assistance to Lebanon,[33] but following the Israel-Hezbollah war in 2006, the Bush Administration requested and Congress appropriated a significant increase in foreign assistance. The war heightened the need for additional economic aid as the Lebanese government and its international and Arab partners vied with Iran and Hezbollah to win the "hearts and minds" of many Lebanese citizens who had lost homes and

---

[32] BBC Monitoring Middle East, "Lebanese UN envoy comments on Security Council membership, Iran sanctions," *Al-Arabiya Television*, May 15, 2010.

[33] In December 1996, the United States organized a Friends of Lebanon conference, which resulted in a total commitment of $60 million in U.S. aid to Lebanon over a five-year period from FY1997 to FY2001 ($12 million per year mainly in Economic Support Funds (ESF)). Congress increased annual aid amounts to $15 million in FY2000 and to $35 million in FY2001, reportedly to help Lebanon adjust to new conditions following Israel's withdrawal from south Lebanon and to help Lebanon cope with continuing economic challenges. U.S. economic aid to Lebanon hovered around $35 million in subsequent years, rising to $42 million in FY2006.

businesses. The war also highlighted the need for a more robust Lebanese military to adequately patrol Lebanon's porous borders with Syria and prevent Hezbollah's rearmament.

Since then, U.S. assistance has been designed to strengthen the institutions of the state to implement UNSCR 1701 and to create alternatives to extremism, reduce the influence and appeal of Hezbollah and other extremist groups and create the political space necessary to allow the government to tackle the range of challenges it faces—from improving fiscal responsibility and environmental resource management to securing its borders and extending the control of the legitimate security forces over the entire territory of the state.

## Economic Support Funds

Economic Support Funds (ESF), administered primarily through USAID, are used for a wide range of activities including programs that support political and economic reform as well as local civil society organizations (CSOs). Lebanon has a robust civil society but sectarian loyalties have resulted in the decentralization of political power, which limits the effectiveness of state institutions and a unifying sense of national identity. U.S. assistance programs are designed to strengthen institutions while at the same time investing in CSOs, education, and various local projects across a range of environmental and infrastructure projects.[34]

ESF funds have also been used to aid in economic recovery following regional and domestic crises. Most recently, the United States committed several hundred million dollars to Lebanon's rebuilding efforts following the 2006 war between Israel and Hezbollah. Then-President Bush announced on August 21, 2006, that the United States would provide an immediate $230 million to Lebanon. At a January 2007 donors' conference in Paris, then-Secretary of State Rice pledged an additional $250 million in cash transfers directly to the Lebanese government. This U.S. economic aid was provided by Congress in the 2007 Emergency Supplemental Appropriations Act (P.L. 110-28).

The cash transfers, funded from the ESF account, are tied to certain benchmarks that the Lebanese government is required to meet. The benchmarks are aimed to encourage economic reform and to lower Lebanon's crippling $43 billion public debt.[35] While a number of the recommended reforms remain outstanding, including reforms in the energy and telecommunications sector, Lebanon has made some progress toward improving its fiscal circumstances.[36] According to the International Monetary Fund (IMF), Lebanon's prudent macroeconomic and financial policies have strengthened the economy's ability to weather external shocks, in spite of large fiscal and external vulnerabilities related to the size of the public debt. Such policies have included the maintenance of fiscal primary surpluses, a cautious interest rate policy, and strict oversight of the financial system. These primary surpluses have contributed to lower the debt-to-GDP ratio by nearly 20 percentage points since 2006. Together, these policies

---

[34] For additional information on current U.S. assistance programs in Lebanon, see the FY2011 Congressional Budget Justification available at http://www.state.gov/documents/organization/137936.pdf.

[35] "Lebanon—2009 Article IV Consultation Mission—Mission Concluding Statement," International Monetary Fund, March 5, 2009. Available at http://www.imf.org/external/np/ms/2009/030509 htm.

[36] The Paris III Conference reform plan is available on the Lebanese Ministry of Finance website at http://www.rebuildlebanon.gov.lb/images_Gallery/Paris%20III%20document_Final_Eng%20Version.pdf.

have helped maintain confidence in the Lebanese economy and financial system, allowing for a steep build-up of international reserves, even during the global financial crisis.[37]

The U.S. also supports Lebanese civil society organizations through the Office of the Middle East Partnership Initiative (MEPI) at the U.S. Department of State. From FY2006-FY2009 Lebanon contributed $23.4 million to civil society programming in Lebanon.[38] There are currently 26 active MEPI projects in Lebanon: 16 multi-country projects including Lebanon; and 10 Lebanon-specific projects. According to MEPI, programming is focused on "supporting the institutions of democracy, especially the parliament and the judiciary; empowering women so that they may assume a more integral role in society; and supporting the growth of the next generation of civil society, governmental and academic leaders."

## Security Assistance[39]

For the first time since 1984, the Administration requested and Congress authorized Foreign Military Financing (FMF) grants to Lebanon in the FY2006 foreign operations appropriations bill. Originally, the request included approximately $1.0 million in FMF for FY2006 and $4.8 million for FY2007 to help modernize the small and poorly equipped LAF following Syria's withdrawal in 2005. However, the summer 2006 war between Israel and Hezbollah spurred Western donors to increase their assistance to the LAF. Drawing from multiple budget accounts, the Administration reprogrammed funds to provide a more robust program of military assistance in order to

> [P]romote Lebanese control over southern Lebanon and Palestinian refugee camps to prevent them from being used as bases to attack Israel. The U.S. government's active military-to-military programs enhance the professionalism of the Lebanese Armed Forces, reinforcing the concept of Lebanese civilian control. To foster peace and security, the United States intends to build upon welcome and unprecedented Lebanese calls to control the influx of weapons.[40]

The FY2007 Emergency Supplemental Appropriations Act (P.L. 110-28, adopted May 25, 2007) included $220 million in FMF for Lebanon, a significant increase from previous levels. Appropriations in FY2008-FY2010 and the FY2011 budget request support these objectives and programs, albeit at lower levels.

On October 6, 2008, the United States and Lebanon established a Joint Military Commission (JMC) to organize their bilateral military relationship.[41] During a JMC meeting on February 12, 2010, Lebanese Minister of Defense Elias Murr and U.S. Assistant Secretary of Defense for

---

[37] "Lebanon—2009 Article IV Consultation Mission—Mission Concluding Statement," International Monetary Fund, March 5, 2009. Available at http://www.imf.org/external/np/ms/2009/030509 htm.

[38] U.S. Consultation with U.S. Department of State, August 3, 2010. This total does not include multi-country projects or regional programs which may include Lebanese participants. For more information on MEPI programs in Lebanon, see http://www medregion mepi.state.gov/lebanon html. MEPI programs are funded through a separate ESF appropriation and do not come out of the bilateral ESF fund.

[39] For additional information, see CRS Report R40485, *U.S. Security Assistance to Lebanon*, by Casey L. Addis.

[40] FY2008 International Affairs (Function 150) Congressional Budget Justification, U.S. Department of State, February 16, 2007.

[41] U.S. Open Source Center (OSC) Document GMP20081007644002, "Washington and Beirut Set up Joint Military Panel," *Daily Star* (Beirut), October 7, 2008.

---

International Security Affairs Alexander Vershbow underscored the long-term, bilateral military partnership between the United States and Lebanon. Following the meeting, the U.S. State Department announced that cooperation efforts in 2010 will have a special focus on the needs of Lebanon's special forces. As of February 2010, the U.S. had provided over $11 million in training and $56 million in sophisticated and specialized equipment for the LAF special forces, including bunker-busting weapons, anti-tank missiles, tactical unmanned aerial vehicles, sniper rifles, night vision devices, and other equipment.[42]

U.S. assistance also supports the Lebanese ISF primarily through International Narcotics Control and Law Enforcement (INCLE) Funding. INCLE funding is used to provide training and equipment to the ISF to enable them to maintain the rule of law while teaching democratic policing techniques and respect for human rights. The current program was started with FY2007 funds with the goal of training 8,000 ISF cadets. INCLE funds are also used to provide training and technical assistance to Lebanese border security services; to develop a secure, nationwide communications network; to support counternarcotics programs; and to strengthen Lebanon's corrections system.[43]

## Budget Transparency

Lebanon is one of 31 countries requiring a waiver for the provision of U.S. assistance. Section 7086(c)(2) of the Department of State, Foreign Operations, and Related Programs Appropriations Act, 2010 (Division F, P.L. 111-117) states that no U.S. assistance may be made available for assistance for the central government of any country that fails to publicly disclose on an annual basis its national budget, to include income and expenditures. The Secretary of State may waive the requirements of paragraph (1) on a country-by-country basis if the Secretary reports to the Committees on Appropriations that to do so is important to the national interest of the United States. Deputy Secretary of State for Management and Resources Jacob Lew signed the FY2010 budget transparency waiver for Lebanon on April 7, 2010.

## Unexploded Cluster Munitions in Lebanon

The Israeli air campaign during the 2006 war against Hezbollah left unexploded ordnances from cluster bombs in Lebanon. The United Nations Mine Action Coordination Center (UNMACC) estimates that 30% to 40% of the estimated 1 million cluster bombs used by Israel failed to explode on impact. Israeli officials acknowledged that most of the weapons used were supplied by the United States. Humanitarian groups have criticized both Israel and the United States for the use of these weapons, which they argue caused extensive and unnecessary civilian casualties during and after the war.[44] Observers as well as some Members of Congress have questions about whether Israeli use of cluster munitions purchased from the United States violates the Arms Export Control Act, and the U.S. State Department has said that it has talked with the Israelis about the matter and issued a preliminary classified report to Congress in January 2007 that Israel

---

[42] http://lebanon.usembassy.gov/latest_embassy_news/press-releases2/pr021310.html.

[43] CRS consultation with U.S. Department of State, July 2010.

[44] Glenn Kessler, "Israel May Have Misused Cluster Bombs, U.S. Says," *Washington Post*, January 30, 2007. The United States has donated $2 million to support ongoing U.N. assisted efforts to clear munitions from southern Lebanon. More information is available at http://www.maccsl.org/.

"may have" misused cluster munitions.[45] A final finding has not yet been issued. Israel has denied violating these agreements, saying that they acted in self-defense.[46]

The international community has contributed to U.N. efforts to clear unexploded ordnances in southern Lebanon. In support of these efforts, the United States contributed $2 million to the voluntary trust fund of the UNMACC. From FY2007 to FY2010, the Congress appropriated a total of $24.65 million in Non-proliferation, Anti-terrorism, De-mining, and Related funding (NADR) for Lebanon, which might also be used in part to support efforts to clear unexploded cluster munitions. The FY2011 budget requested included $4.8 million in NADR funds. Despite these efforts, recent reports indicate that the funding for demining in Lebanon is insufficient to sustain the clearance process through to completion.[47]

# Political Profile

The Lebanese government, with support from the United States and the international community, constantly struggles to maintain the delicate political balance of its confessional system (see "Demography," below). The legacy of civil war and foreign occupation left government institutions weak, and recovery has been difficult, particularly in the face of interference from Iran and Syria through their proxies. Political parties and citizens of Lebanon express both a sense of dissatisfaction with the political system and a reluctance to alter it, possibly because of the national memory of the civil war and a fear that any attempt to alter the political system could reignite the tensions that led the country to fracture along sectarian lines in 1975.

## Demography

Lebanon is among the most religiously diverse society in the Middle East, with 17 recognized religious sects. The Lebanese government operates under a confessional system and government positions are distributed by religion. In 1943, when Lebanon became fully independent from France, leaders of the principal religious communities adopted an unwritten agreement known as the National Covenant, which provided that the president be a Maronite Christian, the prime minister a Sunni Muslim, and the speaker of parliament a Shiite Muslim. Parliamentary seats were apportioned between Christians and Muslims according to a ratio of 6:5, until 1989 when the ratio was evened. Cabinet posts are generally distributed among the principal sectarian communities.

The 1943 ratios were developed based on the sole Lebanese census conducted in 1932 and became less reflective of Lebanese society as Muslims gradually came to outnumber Christians. Within the Muslim community, Shiite Muslims came to outnumber Sunni Muslims.[48] As a result

---

[45] See Transcript from the Senate Appropriations Subcommittee on State, Foreign Operations, and Related Programs Hearing on the 2009 Budget for the State Department, April 9, 2008.

[46] David S. Cloud and Greg Myre, "Israel May Have Violated Arms Pact, U.S. Officials Say," *New York Times*, January 28, 2007.

[47] Bassem Mrou, "U.N. Search for Bombs, Mines in Lebanon Runs Low on Money," *Associated Press*, October 18, 2008.

[48] Because no census has been conducted in Lebanon since 1932, the proportion of Shiite to Sunni Muslims is uncertain. The latest CIA *World Fact Book* estimates state that Lebanon's population is 35% Shiite Muslim, 25% Sunni Muslim, 35% Christian, and 5% Druze and other groups.

of this system, Lebanese political parties developed along religious, geographic, ethnic, and ideological lines and are associated with prominent families. Discontent over power-sharing imbalances was an important factor in the inter-communal tensions and civil strife culminating in the 1975-1990 civil war. These issues are still unresolved.

## Economic Issues and Trade Relations

Lebanon has not adopted a national budget since 2005 and, while the cabinet reported progress on a draft 2010 budget in June 2010, the March 8 opposition continues to reject proposals for tax increases and spending limits supported by the March 14 leadership. A June 2010 International Monetary Fund assessment noted that despite strong economic growth in Lebanon over the last year, public debt (an estimated $51 billion, or 154% of 2009 GDP)[49] is soaring and encouraged the government to implement planned investment in infrastructure while reforming key sectors, such as electricity production.[50] According to the U.S. International Trade Administration, Lebanese exports to the United States in 2009 were $77 million (down from $99 million in 2008) and Lebanese imports from the United States were $1.4 billion (roughly equivalent to the 2008 level).[51]

## Civil War, Occupation, and Taif Reform

At stake in the civil war were control over the political process in Lebanon, the status of Palestinian refugees and militia, and the respective goals of Syria and Israel. From 1975-1990, hundreds of thousands were killed, wounded, or disabled, and comparable numbers were left homeless at one time or another. The war was marked by foreign occupations, kidnappings, and terror bombings. In the aftermath, Lebanon's warring factions reached a precarious consensus, but sectarian divisions and a culture of distrust among Lebanon's various demographic groups persist.

### Syrian and Israeli Incursions

Both Syria and Israel sent troops into Lebanon during the civil war. Syria sent troops into Lebanon in 1976 at the request of then-President Suleiman Frangieh. Israel invaded in 1978 following PLO attacks against Israelis that originated from southern Lebanon.

35,000 Syrian troops entered Lebanon in March 1976 to protect Christians from Muslim and Palestinian militias. From 1987 and June 2001, Syrian forces occupied most of west Beirut and much of eastern and northern Lebanon.

In March 1978, Israel invaded and occupied Lebanese territory south of the Litani River to destroy Palestinian bases that were being used as staging grounds for attacks against Israel. Israeli forces withdrew in June 1978, after the United Nations Interim Force in Lebanon (UNIFIL) was deployed to southern Lebanon to act as a buffer between Israel and the Palestinians (U.N.

---

[49] CRS calculation based on Economist Intelligence Unit 2009 GDP and debt estimates.

[50] International Monetary Fund, Lebanon 2010 Article IV Consultation Mission Concluding Statement, June 9, 2010.

[51] U.S. Department of Commerce, International Trade Administration Office of Trade and Industry Information (OTII), National Trade Data, Custom Report—Lebanon, June 2010. Available at http://tse.export.gov/.

Security Council Resolution 425, March 19, 1978). In June 1982, Israel mounted a more extensive invasion designed to root out armed Palestinian guerrillas from southern Lebanon. Israel defeated Syrian forces in central Lebanon and advanced as far north as Beirut.

Israeli forces completed a phased withdrawal in 1985, but maintained a 9-mile-wide security zone in southern Lebanon from 1985 to 2000. About 1,000 members of the Israeli Defense Forces (IDF) patrolled the zone, backed by a 2,000 to 3,000 member Lebanese militia called the South Lebanon Army (SLA), which was trained and equipped by Israel. Israel withdrew unilaterally from southern Lebanon in 2000, with the exception of its continuing presence in a small area known as the Shib'a farms, which remains disputed.

## Taif Agreement

The Lebanese parliament elected in 1972 remained in place for 20 years because it was impossible to elect a new parliament during the civil war. After a prolonged political crisis, Lebanese parliamentary deputies met in 1989 in Taif, Saudi Arabia, under the auspices of the Arab League, and adopted a revised power-sharing agreement. The Taif Agreement[52] raised the number of seats in parliament from 99 to 108 (later changed to 128), replaced the former 6:5 ration of Christians to Muslims with an even ratio, provided for a proportional distribution of seats among the various Christian and Muslim sub-sects, and left appointment of the prime minister to parliament, subject to the president's approval. In addition, Syria and Lebanon signed a treaty of brotherhood, cooperation, and coordination in May 1991, which called for creating several joint committees and coordinating policies. Although Syrian troop strength in Lebanon reportedly declined over time, Syria continued to exercise controlling influence over Lebanon's domestic politics and regional policies. Syrian intelligence agents also remained active in Lebanon.

The Taif Agreement continues to be the benchmark to which Lebanese people refer in times of stress and sectarian violence. The consensus reached in Taif still guides the distribution of political power in Lebanon. For many in Lebanon, the Taif Agreement is still viewed as the compromise between Sunnis, Christians, and Shiites that keeps the country from falling back into civil war. At the same time, ongoing sectarian violence and political stalemate reflect deep tension over revisiting the core principles of the agreement and the absence of a political framework for reevaluating the distribution of political power in Lebanon.

## Syrian Withdrawal and Parliamentary Elections of 2005

In 2004, tensions mounted between then-Prime Minister Rafiq Hariri, who favored more independence from Syria, and pro-Syrian President Emile Lahoud. On September 2, 2004, the U.N. Security Council adopted Resolution 1559, calling for "all remaining security forces to withdraw from Lebanon," among other things. The next day, the Lebanese parliament, under suspected Syrian pressure, adopted a constitutional amendment that extended President Lahoud's term by three years. Hariri, who disagreed with the amendment, resigned in October 2004 and aligned himself with the anti-Syrian opposition coalition.

---

[52] The full text of the Taif Agreement is available at http://almashriq hiof.no/lebanon/300/320/327/taif.txt.

Hariri was killed when his motorcade was bombed in Beirut on February 14, 2005. Many suspect Syrian involvement in the assassination. His death led to widespread protests by the anti-Syrian coalition including Christians, Druze, and Sunni Muslims and to counter-demonstrations by pro-Syrian groups including Shiites who rallied behind the Hezbollah and Amal parties. Outside Lebanon, the United States and France were particularly vocal in their denunciation of the assassination and of Syria for its suspected role in the bombing.

## Syrian Withdrawal

The Hariri assassination prompted strong international pressure on the Syrian regime, particularly from the United States and France, to withdraw its forces and intelligence apparatus from Lebanon in accordance with Resolution 1559. On April 26, 2005, the Syrian foreign minister informed then-U.N. Secretary-General Kofi Annan and the President of the U.N. Security Council that Syrian forces had completed their withdrawal from Lebanon. The United Nations confirmed that all Syrian troops had been removed but acknowledged allegations that Syrian intelligence still operates in Lebanon and that close, historical ties between the two nations make evaluating the Syrian role in Lebanon difficult.[53]

## Parliamentary Elections of 2005

As Syrian troops departed from Lebanon under U.S. and international pressure, Lebanon prepared to hold parliamentary elections without overt Syrian interference for the first time since 1972. The parliamentary elections, held in four phases between May 29 and June 5, 2005, gave a majority (72 out of 128 seats) to a large, anti-Syrian bloc known as the Bristol Gathering or the March 14 Movement, headed by Saad Hariri, a son of the late prime minister. A second, largely Shiite and pro-Syrian bloc combining Hezbollah and the more moderate Amal organization won 33 seats. A third bloc, the Change and Reform Movement (also known as the Free Patriotic Movement), consisted of largely Christian supporters of former dissident armed forces chief of staff General Michel Aoun,[54] who returned to Lebanon from exile in France in May 2005. Aoun's bloc, which adopted a somewhat equivocal position regarding Syria, gained 21 seats.

Despite Hariri's success, the electoral system resulted in a mixed government, which complicated its ability to adopt clear policies. Hariri associate Fouad Siniora became prime minister, and the 24-member cabinet contained 15 members of Hariri's bloc. It also contained five members of the Shiite bloc, including for the first time in Lebanese history a member of Hezbollah. Other key pro-Syrians remaining in the government were President Lahoud and veteran parliamentary speaker Nabih Berri, who heads the Amal organization (Hezbollah's junior partner in the Shiite coalition). Berri has held the speakership since 1992.

## U.N. Resolutions 1595, 1757, and the Tribunal

On February 25, 2005, the president of the U.N. Security Council issued a statement that condemned the assassination of Rafiq Hariri. On April 7, the U.N. Security Council adopted

---

[53] See U.N. Security Council Document S/2006/832, October 19, 2006, and U.N. Security Council Document S/2007/262, May 7, 2007.

[54] General Aoun (variant spelling: Awn), a controversial former armed forces commander and prime minister, fought against Syria in Lebanon, rejected the Taif Agreement, and eventually obtained political asylum in France.

Resolution 1595 to establish an International Independent Investigation Commission (UNIIIC) in Lebanon "to assist the Lebanese authorities in their investigation of all aspects of this terrorist act, including to help identify its perpetrators, sponsors, organizers, and accomplices." The commission was fully functional as of June 16, 2005.

On May 30, 2007, two years after the commission began its investigation, a divided U.N. Security Council voted 10 to 0 with five abstentions (Russia, China, South Africa, Indonesia and Qatar) to adopt Resolution 1757, which established a tribunal outside of Lebanon to prosecute persons responsible for the attack against Hariri.

Resolution 1757 has proven divisive in Lebanon and elsewhere in the region. Pro-Syrian elements have criticized it and Syria has repeatedly threatened not to cooperate with the tribunal. Opponents of the resolution objected on the grounds that it was passed under Chapter VII of the U.N. Charter, which could include the use of force, and that it represented interference in Lebanon's internal affairs. The Russian delegate to the U.N. commented that "never before has the Security Council ratified agreements on behalf of a parliament of a foreign country."[55]

The United States has contributed $20 million for the tribunal.[56] Lebanon is expected to fund 49% of its costs.[57] For more information, see "Special Tribunal for Lebanon," below.

## Sectarianism and Stability

The strong showing of the March 14 coalition in the 2005 elections and the prospects for stability in Lebanon were soon jeopardized by months of protracted political crises and renewed sectarian violence. From mid-2007 until the agreement in Doha in May 2008, Lebanon's political environment was paralyzed by a number of interrelated disagreements. Preparations for a scheduled September 2007 presidential election went ahead, but were mooted by Lebanese leaders' inability to agree on a consensus presidential candidate and subsequent wrangling over the distribution of cabinet seats. As a result, a vote to elect a new president was postponed until October 23, 2007. Hezbollah and its allies boycotted the balloting and the election was repeatedly delayed as a result. Parties failed to agree on a consensus presidential candidate prior to the expiration of President Emile Lahoud's term in November 2007.

The political stalemate in Lebanon lasted until May 2008, when the worst round of sectarian violence since the civil war broke out in Beirut. On May 6, 2008, Parliament voted to replace the pro-Hezbollah chief of security[58] at Rafiq Hariri International Airport and to dismantle Hezbollah's extensive telecommunications network following accusations that the organization was using these tools to monitor the movement of anti-Syrian politicians. At a press conference on May 8, Hezbollah Secretary General Hassan Nasrallah stated that the cabinet's position was "a declaration of war and a launching of war by the government ... against the resistance and its weapons." A week-long confrontation between Hezbollah and its opposition allies and militias loyal to the Siniora government followed. Shiite protestors burned tires in major thoroughfares,

---

[55] Samar El-Masri, "The Hariri Tribunal," *Middle East Policy*, Fall 2008.

[56] CRS Consultation with U.S. Department of State, July 8, 2010.

[57] U.N. News Service Press Release, "First Official of U.N. Backed Tribunal on Lebanese Killings Starts Work," April 28, 2008.

[58] The chief of security at Beirut airport was a member of the Lebanese Armed Forces (LAF) accused by Druze leader Walid Jumblatt of assisting Hezbollah with monitoring the travel of anti-Syrian diplomats and government officials.

effectively closing the airport. Hezbollah seized control of March 14 coalition strongholds in West Beirut, looting and burning Future Movement media offices.

## Doha Agreement

Fearing continued violence and possibly another civil war, the Arab League and the Qatari government facilitated negotiations between the rival factions. In the resulting "Doha Agreement," the factions committed to end the violence, fill the vacant presidency, arrange for a power-sharing agreement in the cabinet, and hold parliamentary elections in 2009 based on updated electoral laws.

In accordance with the agreement, General Michel Suleiman, perceived as relatively neutral, was elected president on May 25, 2008. He chose Prime Minister Fouad Siniora to continue as the head of the government. Disagreements over the assignment of ministry positions in the cabinet delayed the formation of a unity government until July 11, 2008.

In the new government, Hezbollah and the opposition gained a blocking minority (one-third plus one) of cabinet seats. Eleven ministerial portfolios went to the opposition, including one to Hezbollah itself—the Ministry of Labor. Hezbollah and the opposition have repeatedly pushed for this veto power to block certain government decisions. In particular, Hezbollah has long sought to block any attempt by the government to disarm its militia, as called for in United Nations Security Council Resolution 1701. On August 4, the government released its policy statement to the Lebanese News Agency. Paragraph 24 recognized "the right of Lebanon's people, army and resistance to liberate the Israeli-occupied Shebaa (alternate spelling: Shib'a) farms, Kfar Shuba Hills, and the Lebanese section of Ghajar village, and defend the country using all legal and possible means." It also included the "commitment of the government to United Nations Security Council Resolution 1701 with all its clauses." The policy statement also reaffirmed the government's commitment to hold parliamentary elections in accordance with the Doha agreement.

## Parliamentary Elections 2009

On June 7, 2009, Lebanese voters elected 128 deputies—from 26 districts and 11 politically recognized religious sects—to Lebanon's unicameral legislature. The March 14 coalition won 71 seats to March 8's 57 seats, maintaining its slim majority in parliament.[59]

On November 9, 2009 Minister-designate Saad Hariri announced that consensus had been reached and that a cabinet had been formed. The announcement followed five months of tense negotiations that centered on the minority March 8 coalition's desire to retain the veto power (one-third plus one or 11 of the 30 cabinet seats) that it was granted in the Doha Agreement. Also at issue was the distribution of ministerial portfolios among the parties. Reports indicate that the March 8 coalition fought to keep the Ministry of Telecommunications, which plays an important

---

[59] The March 14 coalition is led by Prime-Minister Designate Saad Hariri and his Sunni party Future Movement. The opposition March 8 Alliance is led by the Shiite party Amal and the Maronite Christian Free Patriotic Movement. It also includes Hezbollah.

role in funding the treasury and in security matters involving surveillance and monitoring communications.[60]

The consensus cabinet is made up of 15 ministers appointed by the majority March 14 coalition, 10 ministers appointed by the March 8 opposition, and five ministers appointed by President Michel Suleiman. This formula differs from the previous cabinet, which provided the March 8 coalition with 11 (one-third plus one) of the 30 ministerial positions and an effective veto over cabinet decisions. The March 8 coalition did retain the telecommunications portfolio, but the Labor Ministry, which was headed by a Hezbollah member in the previous cabinet, went to the March 14 coalition. Hezbollah now holds two ministry positions, the Ministries of Agriculture and Administrative Reform.[61] Some observers have argued that March 8 still holds an unofficial veto in the new cabinet even though it only has 10 seats. The Shiite Minister of State Adnan Hussein, appointed by President Suleiman, reportedly has long-standing ties with Hezbollah and is presumed to be Hezbollah's swing vote on crucial issues.

---

[60] U.S. Open Source Center (OSC) Document GMP20091030644003, "Administrative Problems Delaying Cabinet - Sleiman," *Daily Star Online*, October 29, 2009.

[61] For an overview of the new cabinet, see "Lebanon's New Government," International Foundation for Electoral Systems (IFES) Briefing, November 9, 2009. Available at http://www.ifes.org/publication/ 38e87b372599cdff387c76fd022fb123/Lebanons_new_government.pdf.

# Appendix A. U.S. Assistance to Lebanon

**Table A-1. U.S. Assistance to Lebanon, 1946-2005**

(millions of dollars)

| Year | Total | Economic Aid (Grants) | Food Aid (Grants) | Military Aid (Loans) | IMET (Grants) |
|------|-------|------------------------|--------------------|-----------------------|----------------|
| 1946-1980 | 332.7 | 120.2[a] | 86.2[b] | 123.3[c] | 3.0 |
| 1981 | 24.3 | 4.0 | 0 | 20.0 | 0.3 |
| 1982 | 21.8 | 9.0 | 2.2 | 10.0 | 0.6 |
| 1983 | 153.9 | 52.2 | 0 | 100.0 | 1.7 |
| 1984 | 44.0 | 28.1 | 0.3 | 15.0 | 0.6 |
| 1985 | 21.1 | 19.9 | 0.5 | 0 | 0.7 |
| 1986 | 17.6 | 16.0 | 1.1 | 0 | 0.5 |
| 1987 | 23.0 | 12.8 | 9.7 | 0 | 0.5 |
| 1988 | 12.3 | 5.1 | 6.8 | 0 | 0.4 |
| 1989 | 15.5 | 2.8 | 12.3 | 0 | 0.4 |
| 1990 | 19.4 | 8.3 | 10.7 | 0 | 0.4 |
| 1991 | 19.2 | 9.3 | 9.9 | 0 | 0 |
| 1992 | 16.4 | 9.2 | 7.2 | 0 | 0 |
| 1993 | 14.4 | 10.3 | 3.5 | 0 | 0.6 |
| 1994 | 2.0 | 1.7 | 0 | 0 | 0.3 |
| 1995 | 16.0 | 15.6[d] | 0 | 0 | 0.4 |
| 1996 | 2.5 | 2.0 | 0 | 0 | 0.5 |
| 1997 | 12.8 | 12.3 | 0 | 0 | 0.5 |
| 1998 | 12.6 | 12.0 | 0 | 0 | 0.6 |
| 1999 | 12.6 | 12.0 | 0 | 0 | 0.6 |
| 2000 | 15.6 | 15.0 | 0 | 0 | 0.6 |
| 2001 | 25.5 | 25.0 | 0 | 0 | 0.5 |
| 2002 | 10.7 | 10.1 | 0 | 0 | 0.6 |
| 2003 | 60.3 | 59.6 | 0 | 0 | 0.7 |
| 2004 | 33.9 | 33.2 | 0 | 0 | 0.7 |
| 2005 | 19.6 | 18.8 | 0 | 0 | 0.8 |
| **Totals** | **959.7** | **524.5** | **150.4** | **268.3** | **16.5** |

**Source:** USAID, U.S. Overseas Loans and Grants, http://qesdb.usaid.gov/gbk/.

**Notes:** IMET = International Military Education and Training.

a.   Of the $120.2 million total, $19 million was loans.

b.   Of the $86.2 million total, $28.5 million was loans.

c.   Of the $123.3 million total, $109.5 million was loans and $13.8 million was grants.

d.   Includes about $6 million from 1994.

# Appendix B. Map of Lebanon

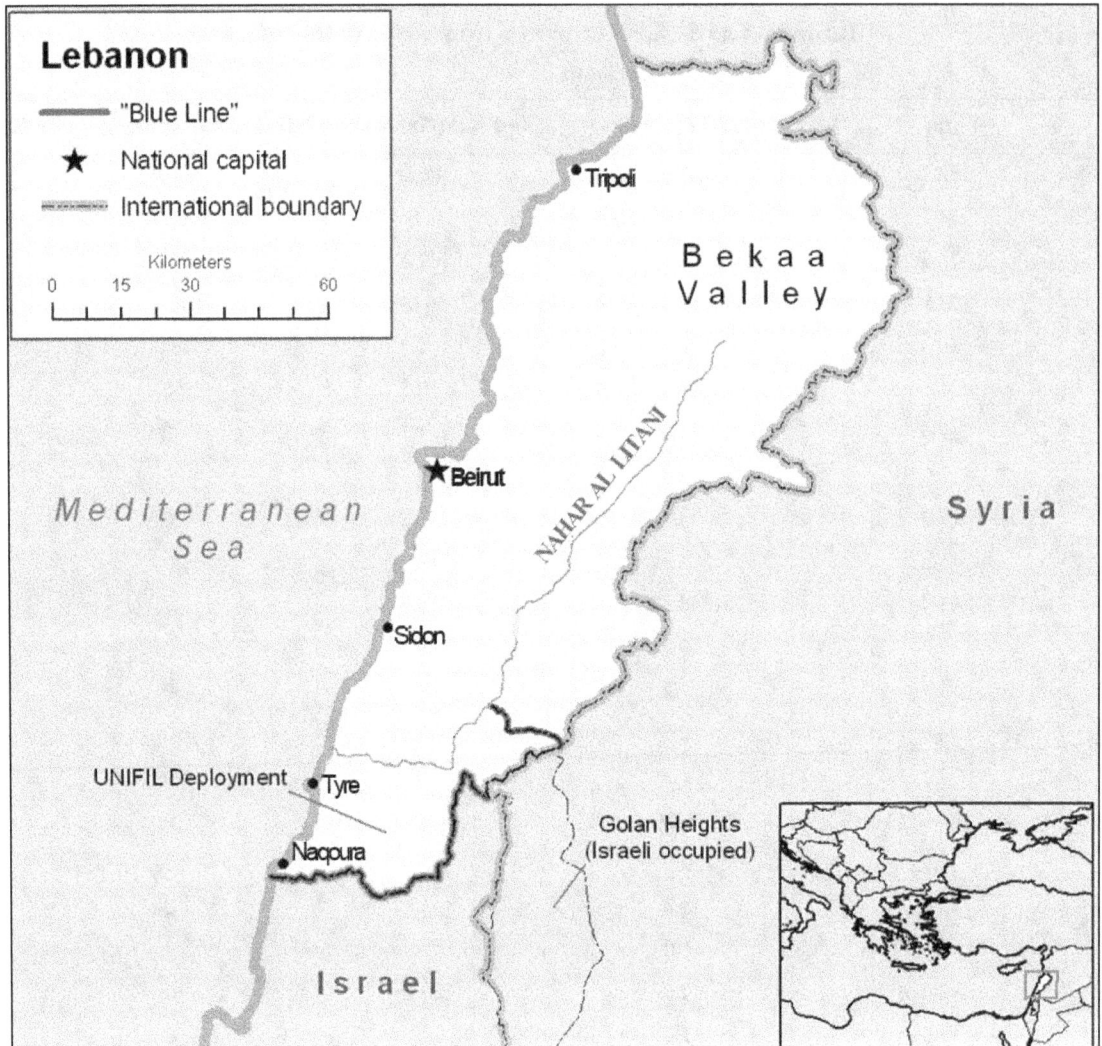

**Source:** Map Resources. Adapted by CRS.

# Author Contact Information

Casey L. Addis
Analyst in Middle Eastern Affairs
caddis@crs.loc.gov, 7-0846

www.ingramcontent.com/pod-product-compliance
Lightning Source LLC
Chambersburg PA
CBHW080759290526
45790CB00008B/3508